Introduction

Hello! and welcome to **Inside Art**, a five-part unit in **The Mix**, the Channel 4 Schools arts series for 7 – 11 year olds.

This series is special because it captures the magic of art. It has been filmed using a stop-frame camera, a special technique which gives the viewer a unique opportunity to follow the development of a piece of art step by step.

Each programme visits the studio of a different contemporary artist who has been specially commissioned to create a 'work of art' for the series. For one month, each artist shared their working practice with the stop-frame camera and we, in turn, share an insight into their ideas, struggles, frustrations, inspirations and techniques. Each produced a finished piece of artwork in different ways, working from varied, diverse sources of inspiration and using a variety of media.

These programmes offer teachers and pupils a chance to share the excitement of seeing a picture being created from concept to completion and to see the subtleties of change and movement in colour, line, tone, form and shape that would be difficult to show in any other way; it is what the medium of television excels in.

We hope that you enjoy the programmes and that the children find them stimulating and informative. Channel Four is always keen to receive comments about the materials and the accompanying support material as well as any children's work.

Please send any correspondence to:

Adrienne Jones
Education Officer, Channel 4 Schools
Educational Television Company
PO Box 100
Warwick
CV34 6TZ

CONTENTS

Inside Art and the curriculum	2
Curriculum grid	3
Points about paints	4
Programme 1 **Martin Jones**	5
Activity page 1: Fishogram	7
Programme 2 **Nicola Bealing**	8
Activity page 2: Design a postcard	10
Activity page 3: Make a sketchbook	11
Programme 3 **Susanna Jacobs**	12
Activity page 4: Mark making – using a pencil	14
Activity page 5: Mark making – lines and textures	15
Programme 4 **Peter Howsen**	16
Activity page 6: Rainbow-colour palette	18
Activity page 7: Tints, shades and tones	19
Programme 5 **Eileen Cooper**	20
Activity page 8: Symbol story	22
Activity page 9: Paint a story	23
Further information	24
Credits	Inside Back Cover
Resources and other relevant series	Insert
Transmission details	Insert

Subtitles
This **Channel 4 Schools** series is subtitled on page 888 of Teletext for the deaf and hearing-impaired. This information is correct at the time of going to press.

Inside Art and the curriculum

Art, craft and design work in schools is enriched through studying the work of artists, craftspeople and designers. **Inside Art** supports this work by reflecting the art curriculum recommendations in England, Wales and Northern Ireland – particularly in relation to skills and understanding – and the expressive arts curriculum in Scotland.

The series shows some of the skills and techniques used by contemporary artists, and the contexts in which they work. Their work reflects the age in which they live just as the work of previous generations of artists did. All five artists featured in the programmes sell their work: sometimes through exhibiting their pictures in galleries, sometimes by having a painting specially commissioned. The series as a whole will help children appreciate that artists have a job, albeit an unusual one.

Throughout the programmes, the artists talk about their work and demonstrate techniques in order to help children make connections with their own artwork and make it possible to take a similar subject as the artist and relocate it within the school environment using comparable materials.

Finding out what different media and materials can do is part of the process of art. Although specially trained, confident and competent, all the artists 'rub out' and amend their work and these programmes are not about showing an end product but following the stages in the journey.

The art of the possible

As preparation for viewing the programmes it would be useful to discuss how an artist might work, what studio space they need and how they prepare to make a painting.

As we see the development of each picture and the difficulties encountered, we are reminded that producing a piece of artwork is not always easy. For children, the programmes show the need to practise and be prepared to make mistakes, redraft and persevere with their efforts. Most of all it will show how this is the working pattern for every artist, that they don't simply throw their first attempt in the bin if it's not what they want.

This series is also about giving the children an opportunity to express themselves, to understand how different artists work and, through this, develop visual literacy – the ability to look at, and understand, a piece of art in order to make informed critical judgements about it.

How to look at a painting

In order to give children practice in ways of looking there are certain questions and activities which can be applied almost universally. These will help to structure children's 'reading' and enjoyment of any painting.

Focus on one or two paintings using view-finders or magnifying glasses. Place a postcard or print of a painting in the middle of a large piece of white paper. In groups, children could talk about the painting – with the teacher perhaps making notes and recording new specialist and descriptive vocabulary as it occurs.

The following are helpful starting-points:

- Look at the technique or 'handwriting' of the artist: Talk about the colours, patterns, the direction of the lines, the thickness or thinness of paint.

- Consider the mood of the painting: How does it make you feel? Is it sad, happy? Do the colours give any clue?

- Look at the overall composition: What has been the viewpoint of the artist? Where has the horizon line been placed? Is the composition 'real' or imagined?

Encourage children to respond to the work using the senses, imagining what it might be like to actually be there in the painting:

What kind of sounds might be heard?

What kind of smells might there be?

If the objects in the painting could be touched, what would they feel like?

Life drawing by Susanna Jacobs

Curriculum grid

Programmes	Content	Outcomes
1 Martin Jones	collecting visual information preparation, sketching using photographs using a range of tools, i.e. sponges, cloth, brushes 'laying on' paint acrylic paints, charcoal	**Art:** texture, tone, colour, backgrounds, working large **English:** vocabulary, poetry **Science:** materials **Music:** rhythm
2 Nicola Bealing	collecting, sorting selecting, planning composition still-life visual diary/travelogue using watercolours and oil paints sketching working outside	**Art:** using a view-finder, setting up still-life, close observation **Geography:** maps **D & T:** designing a postcard, making a sketchbook
3 Susanna Jacobs	figure drawing working with chalk and charcoal exploring line, texture, tone (cubism) redrafting work	**Art:** experimenting with different qualities of line and tone, using charcoal, mark-making **Maths:** shape, line, measurement **Science:** materials
4 Peter Howsen	portrait painting, mood caricature colour mixing development of palette composition building up/destroying	**Art:** mixing colour, making a palette, portraits **Science:** colour, materials **English:** discussion, vocabulary
5 Eileen Cooper	multimedia scale, working large making a canvas working from imagination symbolism collage composition preparation	**Art:** responding to memory and imagination using a range of media, texture **Science:** colour mixing, pigments **Maths:** symbols **English:** story-telling, representation

The process of art

Each programme contains practical elements which are pertinent to work in the classroom. The Teachers' Guide develops these and gives useful suggestions for art skills together with follow-up ideas for English, design and technology, geography and science.

When planning follow-up art activities in conjunction with the **Teachers' Guide**, consider giving children opportunities to work individually, in groups and as a whole class; to work to a big and small scale; to use a broad range of materials; to explore and experiment; to develop ideas and not worry about making mistakes and rethinking ideas; to use sketchbooks; to work from direct observation, memory and imagination; to refer to the work of other artists, designers and craftspeople past and present; to refer to the work of many cultures and to explore work with computers where appropriate.

An artist's studio

Why not set up a studio space in the classroom? It would be an opportunity for groups of children to work as the artists they see in the series. They could also be encouraged to think about what materials and equipment would be needed and how they could be organised.

POINTS ABOUT PAINTS

Powder paint can be used thickly or diluted. It encourages mixing of colours and, if carefully managed, is the cheapest and most versatile medium for painting.

Readymix paint is most suitable for painting large areas and for colours that are difficult to mix such as turquoise or purple.

Acrylic paint dries quickly and permanently. It is made from plastic and has a buttery consistency that will give an opaque, textured surface and can be applied straight from the tube or pot. It can be applied to different surfaces using a stiff brush or diluted with water to give a wash effect. Layers can be applied without smudging, achieving textural surfaces that can also be enhanced by adding sand or salt. It is best to mix on a shiny 'throw away' surface and important to keep brushes moist. (Most suppliers are now producing economical versions of acrylic paints.)

Watercolour paints come in dry cake form or in semi-moist tubes which are very concentrated. They are a useful addition to an art area as they can easily be transported to use outside the classroom. The chief characteristic of watercolour paint is its transparency. Unlike other paints, the watercolour artist must work from light to dark, allowing the paper to shine through. Soft sable brushes are best to give a general wash over a large area, usually on a dampened surface.

Gouache paint and poster paint are opaque and give a matt finish which makes them less luminous and good for detailed work as dark colours can be painted over light ones.

Oil paint is thick and shiny. It is used to paint on canvas, wood or special paper. Oil paint is thinned with turps or mixed with oils and takes a long time to dry. Many artists today work in acrylics as they dry more quickly and give the same glossy quality as oil paints, although oil paint is still the main medium used by artists.

Paint plan

- Have a small amount of good quality materials rather than a cheap mass of inferior ones.

- Have a selection of different kinds of paint available. It is useful to have an agreed uniform colour system throughout the school, eg. lemon, yellow, brilliant yellow, crimson, vermillion, brilliant blue, prussian blue, white. When ordering paint, twice as much white and yellow will be needed.

- Avoid using black paint as this can deaden a painting – mix the three primary colours (red, blue and yellow) – to give a dark grey.

- Arrange the paint area to allow maximum movement without accidents: make sure left-handed children keep their water jars on their left: establish rules about paintbrushes being laid flat rather than left in water pots and general organisation and clearing up procedures.

- Keep the water, brushes, paints clean to keep the paintings bright, remembering that wet paint dries duller.

- Have a good variety of brushes – hog hair, round, chisel shaped, nylon, sable; a chart with the names of the brushes together with the kinds of marks they make will help children to use them appropriately.

- Have a selection of 'other' mark-making tools, such as sponges, rollers, 'made' or collected tools for applying paint and a supply of old rags to take it off!

- Make a small display sheet of different kinds of paper such as cartridge, tissue, poster and brushwork paper and label these to encourage children to select appropriately.

- Vary the size of work, the surface and the sitting or standing positions of the children – (floor, table, wall easel).

- When planning compositions, encourage children to work straight away in paint without drawing first.

- Allow time to talk to the children during their work as well as after. Record any new descriptive or specialist words as they arise.

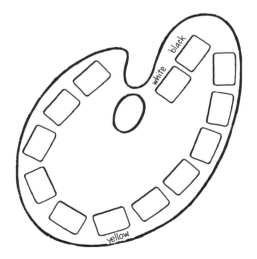

Martin Jones

Programme outline

For this programme Martin Jones paints two pictures. The first one is of an underwater scene using photographs from magazines for inspiration. The paint he uses is acrylic, diluted with water, to make it very runny. He begins by mixing 'watery' colours on a plate and tests out the colours and textures before trying them on the canvas. He makes sketches as part of his preparation and also uses charcoal. The important thing for Martin is the background which he establishes first with sponges and cloths before adding particular detail with a brush.

The second picture he paints is an abstract one which is brought to life before our eyes as he adapts the colour, shapes and figurative detail.

At the end of the programme we see Martin standing in front of the two finished and framed paintings. He tells us he is sometimes quite surprised at his own work!

Learning outcomes

Children should gain an understanding of:

- the process of experimentation to achieve paint effects
- the concept of composition – covering the whole canvas first
- the development of descriptive and specialist vocabulary to respond critically to their own and others' work
- the need for modification and development of an idea to achieve a successful piece of artwork.

Key concepts and vocabulary

Composition ■ Background ■ Texture ■ Detail ■ Colour ■ Consistency

Before viewing

Collecting images

▶ Make a collection of magazine pictures or photographs of imagery related to an underwater scene or another topic such as the rainforest. Sort and categorise by subject, colour and size.

Whilst viewing

Ask the children to note:

- the different ways the artist puts paint on to the canvas
- whether the paint is being applied thickly or thinly, with short or long strokes and with what brushes and tools.

After viewing

Discuss the following with the class:

- What do you think of the artist's work?
- How did he start each picture?
- What sort of colours did the artist use?

"How did you become an artist? I always painted as a child and then went to college.

What sort of things do you think about when you are working on a picture? How the painting is working, and daydream.

How long do you work for each day? Six hours a day, five days a week.

What materials do you like working with best? Oil paints.

Where do you get ideas and inspiration from? I take items from surroundings and streets. Also on a deeper level of consciousness triggered by the process of painting which I don't altogether understand.

What is your favourite colour? Blue.

Is there a piece of work that you would really like to do in the future? Lots of paintings till I drop!"

Fishogram (Activity page 1)

▶ The first of Martin Jones' paintings is an underwater scene. A good way to introduce the theme and encourage all children to be involved is to have a group discussion, recording all the responses. This could take the form of a diagram – like a flow or spider chart – in this case called 'fishogram'.

The 'fishogram' relates to words and ideas associated with an underwater theme and looks at oceans and seas, colours and creatures we might find underwater. Give out the activity page and ask the children, in pairs, to write their word lists in the bubbles provided. This can then lead to poetry or descriptive writing work.

Exploring paint (see also page 4)

In the programme we see Martin Jones creating different background effects using acrylic paint. Creating backgrounds for an underwater theme can be an exciting way to encourage children to explore and experiment with different paint effects using a range of paints.

▶ **Exploring tone** – using powder paint the children could:

- prepare a large sheet of paper by wetting it with a sponge. Mix two different colour paints and with a soft paint brush allow the paint to flow gently on to the paper, letting the colours merge together. See what happens if the paper is held vertically.

- paint a horizon line with a paint brush loaded with runny blue paint. After the first mark, dip into the water pot and continue to make watery lines up to the top of the paper joining one line on to the next. The colour will lighten with each stroke.

- see how many tints of blues or greens they can make by gradually adding white to the colour to make it lighter (add white to the colour, not colour to the white).

- starting with blue as the main colour on the palette, see how many different shades can be mixed. Experiment by gradually adding small amounts of other colours to the blue each time.

▶ **Exploring texture** – using powder paint the children could:

- collect a range of tools other than brushes to make marks with (e.g. scrubbing brushes, toothbrushes, floor mops, rags, sponges). Make painting tools by attaching sponges, twigs, wool or raffia to a stick with tape, string or wire.

- with a good quantity of either blue or green paint, cover a large sheet of white paper with many different marks. Holding the tools in different ways and varying the pressure can achieve different effects. When these sheets are dry they can be used for background and/or torn up for collage work.

- cover a stiff piece of paper or cardboard with a thickish consistency of paint and, while wet, scratch into the surface with tools such as combs. These can be cut from pieces of scrap card to give different thicknesses of line.

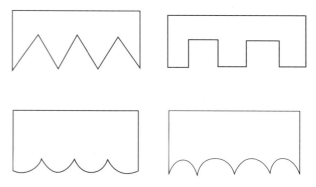

Other textural water effects can be achieved by experiment with marbling, collage work with tissue papers, threads and by monoprinting.

Colour cards

▶ The children could make up a colour chart similar to those produced by paint manufacturers. In groups, they could explore families of colours and then invent their own names for them.

Art with music

▶ Trickle, trickle, splash! Let the children experiment with lines by listening to music and making gestural marks with the brush in time to the rhythm.

Make a mural

▶ Give children the opportunity to work on a large scale and practise the skills related to texture and tone, line and shape. With a limited range of colours, such as blues and greens, make a series of backgrounds – exploring and experimenting with different consistencies of paint, different tools and working in different directions, at different speeds. Use this as a background for a large mural piece adding collections of images such as divers, fish and underwater plants collected from magazines.

Fishogram

▶ Each of the bubbles on this page has a different heading. Under each heading in the bubble write a list of words which go with it. There is an example to start you off.

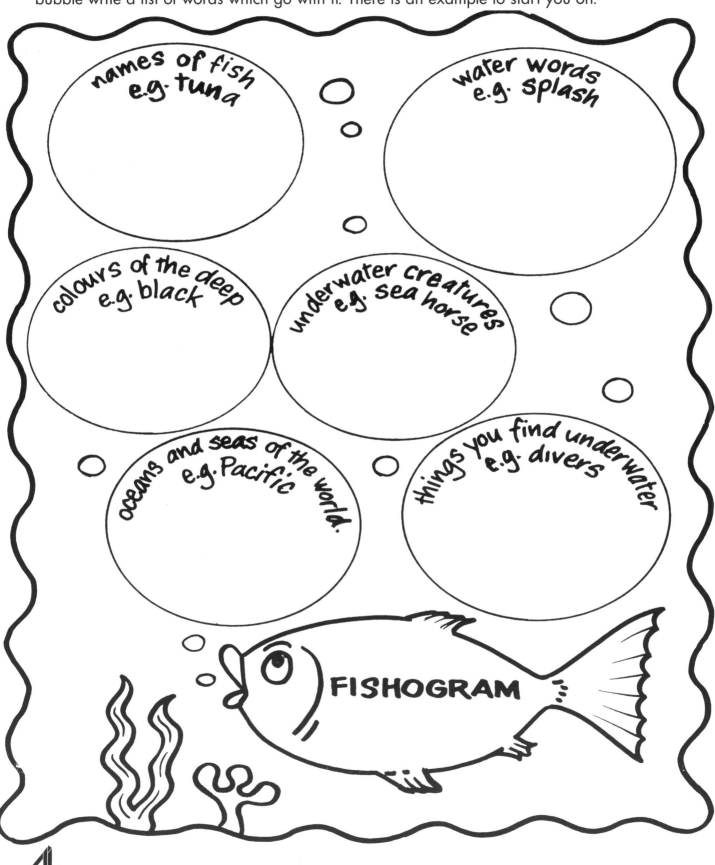

Nicola Bealing

Programme outline

We meet Nicola Bealing in her studio in Cornwall where she has recently returned from her travels in Thailand. Surrounded by beach artefacts, like the crab she paints a still-life of, and mementos from her trip, she prepares to paint scenes from her travels for the purpose of this programme. Nicola works very freely and loosely. All her ideas are brought in from outside and she combines these together in her paintings. The materials she uses include photographs, pencils, watercolours and oils and she paints on card sealed with a coat of emulsion.

A map of the Far East gives us an indication of Nicola's journey and her small painted cameos tell the story of various people and scenes she saw. Whilst away, she carried a small set of watercolour paints and, from rough first drawings, she pieces together the images which she wants to put into her painting. Her work represents a visual journey of her travels.

"How did you become an artist? By going to Art College which included learning a bit about everything from life-drawing to designing cars and then specialising in painting, as it was what I liked best.

What sort of things do you think about when you are working on a picture? Lots of things! The paint and colours and how colours will work together and where things are in the painting and whether things need to be rubbed out and moved around. As a painting progresses, or gets close to being finished I will stand back to look at it – look out of the window, talk to my dog or listen to the radio.

How long do you work for each day? About eight hours, weekends as well usually.

What materials do you like working with best? Oil on primed cardboard or paper. I like using watercolour as well – either in quick sketches or on a large scale with big brushes.

Where do you get ideas and inspiration from? My imagination, daydreaming, eaves-dropping, reading, travelling.

What is your favourite colour? This changes quite often! At the moment a deep, deep dark intense blue."

Is there a piece of work that you would really like to do in the future? A painting that I'm really completely satisfied with – one which starts from a strong idea and in which the drawing, the painting and the colour all pull together to work brilliantly!"

Learning outcomes

Children should gain an understanding of:

- how artists are inspired by many diverse things and that their work takes many forms
- how collecting visual imagery is a constant occupation of artists.

Key concepts and vocabulary

- Shape ■ Colour ■ Composition ■ Still-life
- Landscape Section

Before viewing

Map work

▶ Encourage the children to use atlases to see where a) Cornwall is and b) Thailand, where Nicola Bealing went on her travels.

Collections

▶ Most people collect things. Find out what variety of objects and artefacts the children in the class collect.

Whilst viewing

Ask the children to note:

- how the objects and artefacts are arranged in this artist's work
- how the artist uses photos and sketches as inspiration for her composition
- how the artist paints a frame around the edge of her painting before she starts.

After viewing

Discuss the following with the class:

- What do you think of the artist's work?
- What do you think inspired the artist to make this painting?
- Why did the artist sketch as well as take photographs?

Still-life

Look at two or three contrasting still-life paintings and discuss what a still-life picture is. What objects are used? How are they arranged?

Collecting things

▶ Most people collect objects and artefacts. People often collect unusual items that have a particular meaning for them or remind them of a visit or past event. Artists often use their collections as inspirations for artwork.

Ask the class about the kinds of things that they collect (e.g. photographs, stamps, labels, foreign coins, pottery). Develop a class 'museum' of interesting objects and begin to catalogue the collection.

Design a postcard (Activity page 2)

▶ Postcards are a good item to collect. Ask the children to imagine that they are on a day trip or on holiday and are going to send a postcard to someone who specially collects them. Give out the activity page and explain how to complete it.

Make a view-finder

▶ This is a useful device to help focus on a small area of a painting or drawing when planning a composition and can be made using card from cereal boxes. Let children cut a square or rectangle from the middle of the card leaving a wide border. Two 'L' shapes will give a flexible frame that can be moved in and out to encompass a section of the work.

Setting up a still-life

▶ Collecting, selecting and arranging objects for a still-life can be an interesting art activity on its own. Put a collection of still-life objects together according to a theme, such as similar colours, or shapes or items with patterns on. Choose objects of different lengths, heights and widths and include both angular and curved shapes.

When planning out the composition, look at the objects as basic forms such as spheres, cylinders, cubes or cones. This will help to see the objects as shapes rather than things. Look at the composition from several angles.

▶ In pairs, ask the children to practise setting up still-life groups. They should choose objects with a similar or a contrasting theme. These could be natural objects such as plants, fruits, fish, bones or made objects such as domestic items, personal possessions, clothes or artefacts from different cultures. Be careful not to choose too many objects and vary the size, texture, shape and tone.

Painting a still-life

▶ Suggest that the children set up a 'red' or 'green' still-life, collecting together items of the same 'hue'. 'Green' might comprise a cucumber, pullover, jug, leaves. Encourage the children to use a view-finder and then mix up a key colour, sketching in the objects very lightly at first, using a floppy brush. Emphasise that mistakes do not matter and, like Nicola Bealing does in the programme, can be painted over.

Make a sketchbook (Activity page 3)

We see Nicola Bealing using her sketchbook to record scenes from her travels. Sketchbooks are a vital part of an artist's work. They can contain anything and everything: experiments with different materials, studies from nature, plant life, buildings, imaginative work developed from stories, poems, music, dreams and fantasies or collections of things such as labels, photographs and magazine cuttings.

▶ Set each child in the class the task of making a simple sketchbook from a single sheet of paper by following the instructions on the activity page.

▶ Encourage the children to make small sketches of one spot from their route around the school. They could then put these images together to make a 'comic strip' visual journey. Alternatively, photographs could be used for this activity.

Working on location

Whether the children are sketching in a museum or gallery or simply adding to their visual diary by making sketches in the school grounds, it is useful to prepare the materials and equipment needed in advance.

Plastic wallets, that can double up as a container for pencil sharpenings, could be filled with clipboards, sketchbooks, a range of lead and coloured pencils, pens for making notes and 'looking devices' such as magnifying glasses and view-finders.

▶ Ask the children to make sketches of three examples of textures (trees, brickwork, roofs), shapes within shapes such as windows in walls plus notes about the colours they see. Encourage them to sit comfortably and make quick sketches, gathering information quickly rather than spending too long on one aspect of the scene.

Activity page 2

Design a postcard

Imagine that you have gone somewhere special for the day, or you might even be on holiday. Design this postcard to send to your friend or member of your family.

▶ Draw or paint the image for the front of the postcard here

▼ Write what you want to say here   ▼ Write the address of the person you are sending it to here

10 © 1995 The Educational Television Company Limited

Inside Art Nicola Bealing

4 SCHOOLS

Make a sketchbook

▶ The diagrams on this page show you how to make a mini sketchbook from a single sheet of paper. It can be any size.

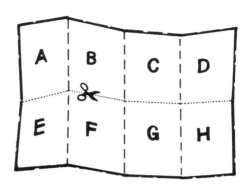

1 Fold the sheet in four where the dashed lines are and cut along the dotted line.

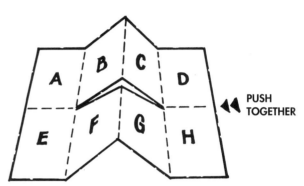

2 Push the ends so the fold in the middle sticks up.

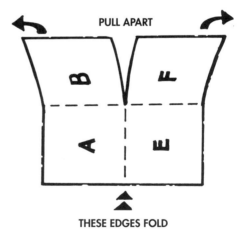

3 Turn it round to face you and pull the pieces marked B and F apart.

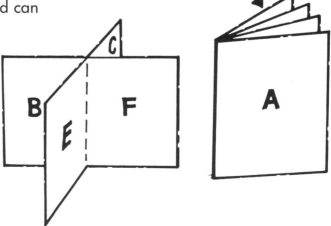

4 The book now makes a cross-shape and can be folded to make double-sided pages.

Inside Art Nicola Bealing   © 1995 The Educational Television Company Limited

Susanna Jacobs

Programme outline

Susanna Jacobs specialises in life-drawing using chalk, charcoal and a rubber in her work. She shows how to use these materials to best effect with different kinds of lines, rubbing out and smudging.

Inspired by the work of Matisse, what Susanna is most interested in is not photographic likeness but how to best capture the structure of sitters. She likes to get a 3D look. In this programme she uses two sitters and each one poses for three-quarters of an hour at a time.

One of the problems of life-drawing is the difficulty for the person being drawn to remain absolutely still all the time. But for Susanna this is what is most exciting and it results in the artist constantly changing the shape, line and form of the drawing so that what is created is the space in and around the lines which gives an almost skeleton-like portrayal of the sitter.

"How did you become an artist? By having the ambition to become one, and by working hard. I went to art school, looked at the work of other artists that I admired, talked to friends who were also excited by drawing and painting and most importantly I set up my own studio where I can concentrate on developing my own work.

What sort of things do you think about when you are working on a picture? Mainly about ways to tackle the problems which I come up against while making a picture.

How long do you work for each day? Between four and five hours.

What materials do you like working with best? Drawing materials especially charcoal and chalks.

Where do you get ideas and inspiration from? From looking at the person who is modelling for me, from the picture as it evolves and from other paintings, drawings and sculptures that I admire.

What is your favourite colour? Blue, brown and grey.

Is there a piece of work that you would really like to do in the future? Yes, a vast painting or drawing of objects that I am gradually collecting in my studio."

Learning outcomes

Children should gain an understanding of:

- exploring line and tone, using charcoal and other drawing media
- the fact that continuous redrafting, looking and re-looking is an important part of an artist's work.

Key concepts and vocabulary

- Life-drawing ■ Movement ■ Tone ■ Profile
- Pose ■ Sitter ■ Sketching ■ Redrafting texture

Before viewing

▶ Explore charcoal effects by encouraging the class to make some experimental marks on a large sheet of brushwork paper using charcoal. Include rubbing-out.

Whilst viewing

Ask children to note:

- how the artist looks at her subject when she works
- how the artist rubs out and alters her work
- the different kinds of lines and marks are used in the picture.

After viewing

Discuss the following with the class:

- What do you think of the artist's work?
- Why do you think the artist works the way she does?
- What kind of materials does the artist use in her work?

Mark making – using a pencil
(Activity page 4)

In the programme we see the artist working with charcoal. Practising mark making using a range of pencils first will help children develop drawing skills that can be used later with charcoal.

Pencils range from very hard graphite to soft sketching pencils. Softer pencils are graded from B to 7B (softest) and hard pencils from H to 6H (hardest). Soft pencils are best for sketching but wear down quickly and it is important to keep them sharp.

▶ Encourage the children to investigate the grading of pencils by making marks with each one and recording the grades (usually found at the end of the pencil).

▶ Give out the activity page and ask children to practise making lines on a separate piece of paper using a range of different lead pencils and then felt pens. Encourage them to fill the whole page.

▶ When they have practised this they could then take a line for a walk without taking the pencil off the paper. This can be done individually, in pairs or groups with one person giving instructions for the line, e.g. move the line to the right, make it a broken line, turn left, make the line curve upwards.

Other drawing tools

Lay out a range of drawing tools. These can include coloured pencils (some that can be used with water), felt pens, ink pens, biros, chalks, pastels and charcoal.

▶ In groups, working on a large sheet of white brushwork paper, allow the children to practise making different kinds of marks using a range of drawing tools. Hold the medium in different ways, at the top, middle, bottom, rolling it between fingers, putting pressure at the point, on the side or by smudging. Work in different directions up, down, across, diagonal, round. Talk about the kinds of marks and ask the children to note how gently or hard they are pressing, whether their marks were made quickly or slowly.

▶ Allow the children to also practise with white chalk on black paper or with a large black felt pen on newsprint.

Story-telling

▶ This can be an interesting way of practising mark-making and language together. Children could work in pairs, one speaking, the other drawing, to tell stories using lines and dots. For example, 'One day a line woke up, shook itself lazily and suddenly realised it was late for a meeting with an exclamation mark. The line hurried along but got lost and went round and round in circles until it met a comma which told it to turn right...'

Mark making – tone, line and texture
(Activity page 5)

▶ Give out the activity page and encourage children individually, to practise using lines to create tone, shade and texture.

Charcoal

Charcoal is one of earliest materials, first seen used in cave drawings made with burnt twigs. Until the early fifteenth century charcoal drawing was used as preparation for a painting by artists. Later it was still used by artists such as Dürer and Rembrandt.

Charcoal comes in compressed sticks of different thicknesses. Best effects are achieved on a roughish surface such as brushwork paper. Charcoal has particular qualities but it is not a good medium for small detailed work.

Holding the stick of charcoal by the fingertips avoids smudging. Broad tonal areas can be made by using the stick of charcoal on the side or smudging with fingers or pieces of tissue. Working with speed and to a large scale achieves best results.

Charcoal pencils, although not as 'loose' to work with, are a useful alternative to charcoal sticks as the charcoal is encased in wood.

Because it can be rubbed out and corrected easily, mistakes do not matter and re-drafting can often enhance the drawing.

Charcoal can be sprayed with fixative or hair spray to stop it smudging and it is useful to protect finished drawings with tissue paper. Often considered a 'messy' material, charcoal is easily cleaned off.

Using charcoal

▶ In pairs, ask children to practise using charcoal to explore tonal contrasts, i.e. light and dark areas. Children can smudge using fingers, thumbs or small pieces of tissue to create tones of grey.

▶ Drawing with charcoal can be about 'taking away' as well as adding. Ask children to cover an area of paper with a solid area of charcoal and to use a pencil-shaped eraser to 'draw' by taking areas of dark away.

▶ Work on a large scale where possible; children can work on a large roll of poster paper or a wallpaper roll laid on the floor. They could draw round each other with thick lines, move position and redraw. These outlines will give a sense of movement and can be left as line drawings.

Mark making – using a pencil

▶ See what different kinds of marks you can make by holding a pencil in different ways. Try the following:

short, angry marks

gentle, smooth, flowing marks

long flowing lines

fussy lines

wobbly, curvy lines

straight lines with wobbly ones on top

lines that bump into each other, wrap around each other and then open out

lines that wind around each other

On a clean piece of paper

▶ Close your eyes and draw some of these lines from memory.

▶ Take a line for a walk by making it swirly, zig-zag, curvy, squiggly, bumpy, scribbly, spiral, wavy and broken.

▶ Make a drawing of a person without taking your pencil off the paper.

Mark making – lines and textures

Here are some examples of how to use lines to fill in shade and texture.

▶ Use the tip of a pen or a pencil and on a blank piece of paper, copy the examples on this page. Then experiment on your own.

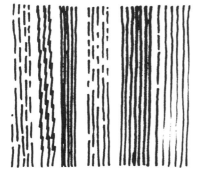 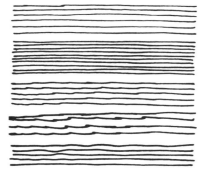 

vertical lines with lines drawn close together and then further apart

horizontal lines

curved lines drawn very quickly

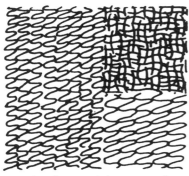 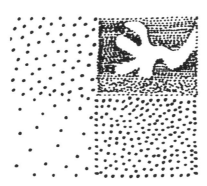 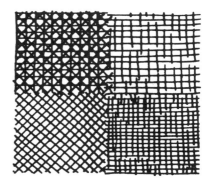

cross hatching with lines very close together and on top of each other

dots of different sizes with larger or smaller spaces between them

small zig-zag lines close together

▶ On the grid below, fill each box with different texture marks. Make up a name to describe the different kind of marks you have made.

Inside Art Susanna Jacobs

Peter Howsen

Programme outline

Peter Howsen is the official war artist for the UK and internationally famous. For the programme he was asked to paint a self-portrait. He decided to paint two pictures of himself that echoed different moods – the 'Jekyll and Hyde' of his nature. Peter shows how different moods can be created through the use of colour and we see him 'destroying' the painting over and over as he changes the colours and style.

He talks about the qualities of the paint he uses. Peter works in oils and likes to organise his oil colours formally on the palette. This means he lays out the colours in the spectrum of the rainbow because this way, they mix very well. For him, painting is a journey and art is an obsession; it is an activity where he is learning all the time.

"**How did you become an artist?** My grandmother gave me a set of oil paints at the age of four. Later I went to Art College.

What sort of things do you think about when you are working on a picture? The research I've done and the colours I'm using and how I feel at the moment.

How long do you work for each day? I work about eight hours a day starting early at about 7 a.m.

What materials do you like working with best? Oil paint on canvas.

Where do you get ideas and inspiration from? People around me, faces and local characters.

What is your favourite colour? Turquoise, green and red.

Is there a piece of work that you would really like to do in the future? The entire set design for a Don Giovanni opera."

Learning outcomes

Children should gain an understanding of:

- colour and the development of the artist's palette
- how painting a self-portrait involves getting to know your own face and moods closely.

Key concepts and vocabulary

- Self-portrait
- Composition
- Viewpoint
- Expression
- Tone
- Pigment
- Palette

Before viewing

Ourselves

▶ Artists have always used themselves as models and painted self-portraits at different times in their life, capturing a moment in time in the same way as a photograph does. Ask the children to make a collection of pictures of themselves as a baby. Compare these with photos of how they look today.

Artists' pictures

▶ Visit a gallery and encourage children to focus on two self-portraits. Make comparisons between them. List the differences in the use of colours and the mood of the painting. Can the children tell how the artist is feeling? (Often the eyes can give a clue.)

Whilst viewing

Ask the children to note:

- how often the colours change in Peter's two self-portraits
- how the head changes position from side to front view and slightly turned. This is all because of the stop-frame camera.

After viewing

Discuss the following with the class:

- What do you think of the artist's work?
- Why do you think Peter Howsen kept changing his painting?
- Can you remember some of the colours the artist used?

Rainbow-colour palette (Activity page 6)

Picasso once said that it sometimes hurt him 'to throw away a palette because it often ended up a good painting'.

▶ Give out copies of the palette on the activity page. Encourage the children to make their own palettes like Peter Howsen's in the programme. They are asked to complete the palette with a range of colours which mirror all the colours in the rainbow. They can use paint, samples of colour from magazines or even a household paint colour chart.

Pigments

Most colours are made from things in the natural world: plants, earth, rocks, precious stones and metals – even dried bodies of insects. Raw materials have to be ground to a powder called pigment and mixed with a medium called binder to make them liquid. This can be water, oil, gum (from trees and plants), glue or eggs. Pigments can sometimes be very expensive and have unusual names. Throughout history the artist's palette has altered as new technologies have been developed.

▶ By looking at a range of different paintings over time, can the children try to re-create the colour palettes of other painters, e.g. Rembrandt, Rousseau.

What materials?

▶ In groups, ask the children to design a catalogue of the art, craft and design materials and equipment in the classroom or school. Each group could take different materials, e.g. paper and brushes, paint and tools. Encourage the children to use specialist vocabulary and note against each item the most appropriate materials for different kinds of work.

Tints, shades and tone (Activity page 7)

▶ Give out the activity page. It looks at the difference between tone and shade. Discuss this with the class and ask them to follow carefully the instructions on the page to see what happens. If the three primary colours are mixed it will make grey. Adding complementary colours will make grey. Tones are somewhere between colour and grey.

▶ Peter Howsen tells us that he uses white, yellow ochre, light red, and a touch of green and black to make flesh tones. We all have different flesh tones. Through careful observation and discussion with a partner, how many flesh tones can the children create using paint and white paper? Testing a small blob of colour (like make-up) on the hand is a good way to check accuracy. Encourage them to keep a note of how the colour was actually made.

Here's looking at you!

▶ Make a display and discuss faces from different times and places. Talk with the class about colours, composition, materials, expression, caricature and cartoon drawings.

▶ Ask the children in pairs to describe each other's faces. What happens to the face, (eyes nose etc.) when feeling happy, sad, angry, worried? Study different expressions. Introduce the class to the detail of how to draw a face by asking them to consider the following points:

Get to know the face by feeling it and measuring parts of it with the fingers. Feel where it curves round and where all the features are.

- Look closely at the face in a mirror.
- Are the two eyes exactly alike or slightly different?
- Are the eyes more or less one eye-width apart?
- What is the shape of the lower lid?
- Where is the darkest shadow?
- Is the mouth nearer the nose or the chin?
- How does the face change when you turn your head?

▶ Get the children to look at the whole face. Take measurements by closing one eye and placing a pencil against the mirror to gauge the distance. There is no substitute for really looking. Spend more time looking at the model than the paper. Draw what is seen and not what is imagined!

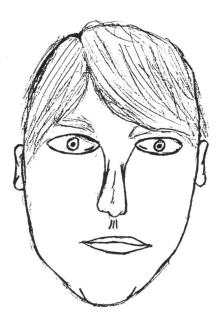

Rainbow-colour palette

Artist Peter Howsen uses a palette shaped like this to mix his paints on.

The paints follow round the palette in the order of the rainbow and the names of some of the colours have been written down but all the colours are missing.

▶ Can you put colour in all the empty spaces? Use paint very carefully or cut out colours from a magazine and stick them on. Make up some names for the colours that don't have them and write them on the palette.

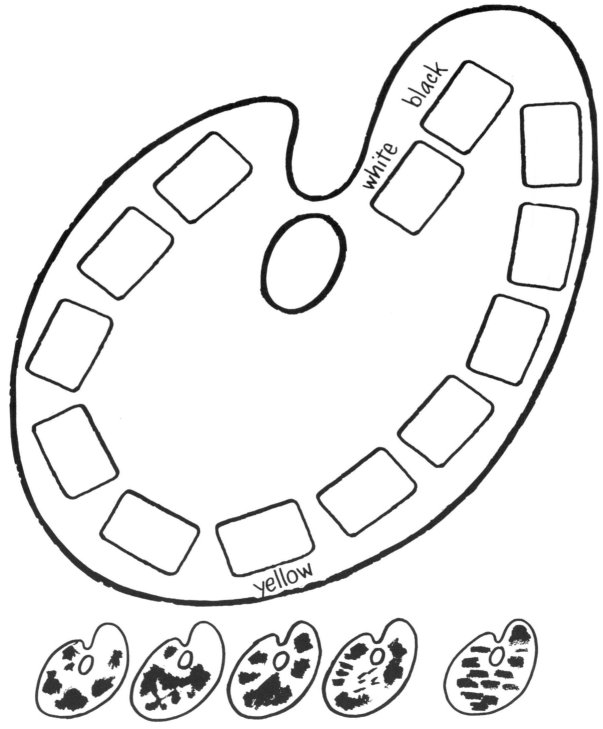

Inside Art Peter Howsen

Tints, shades and tones

1 Tints are made when you add white to a colour.

▶ Choose one colour to use and add a small amount of white each time until you finish with white.

2 Shades are made when you add black to a colour.

▶ Use the same colour as before and add a small amount of black each time until you finish with black.

3 What happens to the colour when you

▶ Start with red and follow the instructions below

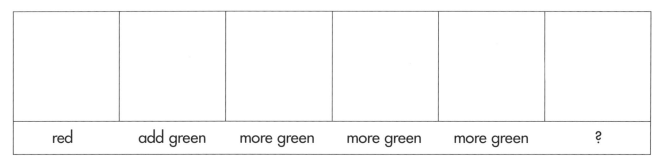

| red | add green | more green | more green | more green | ? |

▶ Start with blue and follow the instructions below

| blue | add orange | more orange | more orange | more orange | ? |

Inside Art   Peter Howsen

Eileen Cooper

Programme outline

Eileen Cooper is an art teacher who uses a wide variety of materials in her work. She loves experimenting to see how different materials behave when used together and she never worries about ruining her pictures. According to her, the more risks that are taken, the better.

For her own large-scale paintings she favours thinned, runny oil paint and often puts her canvases on the floor and lets the transparent paint move where it wants to.

Her paintings tell stories and are full of bright colours. In this programme she uses swirls like Catherine wheels to start her pictures. There is no perspective in her work but strong use of symbols which she practises drawing beforehand. If people are big in Eileen's paintings it is because they are important. If they are red it might be that they are angry.

"How did you become an artist? I went to Art School.

What sort of things do you think about when you are working on a picture? Colour, imaginary and normal things. Kids, feeding the kids and the washing.

How long do you work for each day? Five hours maximum.

What materials do you like working with best? Various, oil on canvas, charcoal on paper and collage.

Where do you get ideas and inspiration from? Life.

What is your favourite colour? Red and blue.

Is there a piece of work that you would really like to do in the future? Ceramics.**"**

Learning outcomes

Children should gain an understanding of:

- the fact that paintings can often be used to tell a story. (Narrative is a rich theme in art – from religious paintings to contemporary comic strip or video and film.)
- the idea that paintings can be used to express feelings and moods
- the idea that colours are often used symbolically in art.

Key concepts and vocabulary

- Primary colours ■ Brightness ■ Viewpoint
- Scale ■ Composition ■ Abstract ■ Mixed media
- Symbol ■ Transparent

Before viewing

Symbol story (Activity page 8)

▶ Give the children copies of the activity page and without giving them any clues, encourage them to think about what the four different images suggest to them.

Abstract art

▶ Abstract compositions use symbols to represent people, things and feelings. As a class, look at some examples of abstract pictures and talk with the children about:

- what is happening in the picture
- who the people are and what they are doing
- what the other images in the picture represent.

Whilst viewing

Ask the children to note:

- what kinds of images the artist chooses for her compositions
- how many different media the artist uses in one piece of work
- how she alters the parts of the painting she is not happy with.

After viewing

Discuss the following with the class:

- What do you think of the artist's work?
- What do you think inspired the artist to make this painting?
- What colours did the artist use?

Symbol story (Activity page 8)

▶ Ask the children to cut or tear out, or copy the four shapes on the activity page. Using a blank sheet of A4 paper, see how many different arrangements they can make. Once they have explored the ideas of size, direction and space they can then stick their composition down and maybe add extra images and colour.

▶ Photocopy several versions of the same symbol composition. Ask the children to experiment to see how exactly the same picture can change the effect it has simply by changing the colours in it.

Exploring line

▶ Individually suggest that the children make some 'magic' swirling, wavy lines using a candle and with very diluted ink or paint. They could then wash over the surface of the wax using a floppy brush to see where the wax will resist the colour.

Paint a story (Activity page 9)

These short, visual stories can help children explore abstract paintings and understand how a story can be told with colours and shapes. They can be as simple or as complicated as appropriate. Children can guess what each other's stories are and go on to invent others of their own.

▶ Make several photocopies of the activity page. Cut them up into sections and give each child one section to make into a painting. Alternatively, the children could be given their own activity page complete and make their own choices.

The emotion of colour

▶ Help children to develop a feeling about colour by talking about different states and how they can be associated with colour, e.g. 'I've got the blues'. Then ask children, in groups, to group a range of colours into warm, happy, sad, angry, irritating, calming.

Colour weaving

▶ Using a range of different materials of different textures, ask the class to weave these together, with 'hot' colours horizontal and 'cold' colours vertical.

Mixed media

▶ Using the full range of materials available in the classroom, allow the children, in small, controlled groups, to experiment with combining different media in the same way as Eileen Cooper does in the programme, e.g. paint a wash and sprinkle powder paint or food colouring on to it whilst still wet.

▶ Encourage the children to explore how thickly they can mix powder paint by adding PVA or flour and water paste. Experiment using a stiff brush or a spatula to push the paint around on the paper. A small quantity of dry powder paint, sand or earth can also be added at this stage to give a textural effect.

Making paints

Let the children experiment with making their own paints.

They will need pigment and binder. Pigments can be made using a ground-up chalk, charcoal, soot or spices; binder can be made using a teaspoon of cooking oil, egg white, egg yolk, honey or linseed oil.

Method

▶ Grind the powder with the back of a spoon, add the binder and mix the ingredients together evenly. The colours produced will all be shades of grey but different binders will create a variation of tone.

Art from words

▶ In response to the stimulus of a poem or short story, encourage the class to create a picture representing the words with different symbols.

Symbol story

▶ Look at the shapes on this page. Cut or tear them out. Now arrange them on a clean sheet of paper. Try moving them around until you like the way they look and then stick them down.

Inside Art Eileen Cooper

Paint a story

▶ Choose one or two stories from the following list. Read them carefully. Don't tell anyone which ones you have chosen.

▶ Mix up some powder paints according to the colours in the story. On a blank sheet of paper use the paint to tell the story. Try to follow the instructions exactly.

1 Four red circles bump into green squiggly lines in the middle of the paper. They dance around in a circle and move together before they fall downwards, gradually turning into dots at the bottom of the paper.

2 Five yellow triangles sit on one edge of the paper. Three large squares of different colour red overlap in the middle. They slowly turn into small orange triangles that float to the edge of the paper to meet the yellow triangles.

3 Four different green blobs are surrounded by a bubbling red sea of small squiggles and waves.

4 Two big blue circles get lighter around their edges. Six red oval shapes of different sizes move into the middle from the corners.

5 Red and yellow wavy lines of different thicknesses swim across the paper. They go through a blue river from left to right and back again.

▶ Now make up one of your own.

4 SCHOOLS   Inside Art   Eileen Cooper   © 1995 The Educational Television Company Limited   **23**

Further information

Places

Aberdeen – **Art Gallery**
01224 646333

Bath – **Victoria Art Gallery**
01225 352124

Birmingham – **City Museum & Art Gallery**
0121 235 2834

Bradford – **The Colour Museum**
Perkin House
82 Grattan Road
Bradford BD1 2JB
01274 390955

Bristol – **Arnolfini**
0117 9299191

Bristol – **City Museum & Art Gallery**
0117 9223571

Cambridge – **Fitzwilliam Gallery**
01223 332993

Cardiff – **National Art Gallery**
01222 397951

Eastbourne – **Towner Art Gallery**
01323 725112

Glasgow – **Museum**
0141 357 3929

Leeds – **City Art Gallery**
0113 2478264

Liverpool – **Tate Gallery**
0151 709 3223

Manchester – **City Art Gallery**
0161 236 5244

Oxford – **Ashmolean**
01865 278000

Oxford – **Museum of Modern Art**
01865 722733

Powys – **Museum of Modern Art**
01654 703355

St Albans – **City Museum**
01727 819339

St Ives – **Tate Gallery**
01736 796545

Sheffield – **Mappin Gallery**
0114 2726281

Southampton – **City Art Gallery**
01703 223855

Tenby – **Museum & Picture Gallery**
01834 842809

London –

British Museum 0171 636 1555

Commomwealth Institute 0171 603 4535

Courtauld Institute 0171 873 2620

Dulwich – Picture Gallery 0181 693 6911

National Gallery 0171 8393321

National Portrait Gallery 0171 306 0055

Tate Gallery 0171 887 8000

Victoria & Albert Museum 0171 938 8500

Books

Approaches to Art, Anthea Peppin & Ray Smith pub. Ginn

Art in Practice, Margaret Morgan pub. Nash Pollock Publishing

Drawing to Learn Dawn & Fred Sedgewick pub. Hodder & Stoughton

Education for Art, Rod Taylor pub. Longman

What is Art?, Rosemary Dickinson pub. OUP

Primary Art, pub. Folens (Dunstable) 01582 472788

Primary Art, Bob Clements & Shirley Page pub. Oliver Boyd

Royal Academy of Arts: Painting, Elizabeth & Anne Harris pub. Dorling Kindersley

Sketchbooks: Explore and Store, Gillian Robinson pub. Hodder & Stoughton

Start with Art, Su Fitzsimmons pub. Simon and Schuster

A Teachers Guide to Learning from Objects, Gail Durbin, Susan Morris & Sue Wilkinson pub. English Heritage

Understanding Modern Art, Monica Bohm-Duchen & Janet Cook pub. Usborne

Water Colour: Eyewitness Art, Michael Clarke pub. Dorling Kindersley